AF417206

UNDERSTANDING AND DEVELOPING EMOTIONAL INTELLIGENCE

WHAT IS EMOTIONAL INTELLIGENCE, WHY IT MATTERS, AND HOW TO DEVELOP IT.

BHARATH ULLIKASHI

Copyright © Bharath Ullikashi
All Rights Reserved.

This book has been self-published with all reasonable efforts taken to make the material error-free by the author. No part of this book shall be used, reproduced in any manner whatsoever without written permission from the author, except in the case of brief quotations embodied in critical articles and reviews.

The Author of this book is solely responsible and liable for its content including but not limited to the views, representations, descriptions, statements, information, opinions and references ["Content"]. The Content of this book shall not constitute or be construed or deemed to reflect the opinion or expression of the Publisher or Editor. Neither the Publisher nor Editor endorse or approve the Content of this book or guarantee the reliability, accuracy or completeness of the Content published herein and do not make any representations or warranties of any kind, express or implied, including but not limited to the implied warranties of merchantability, fitness for a particular purpose. The Publisher and Editor shall not be liable whatsoever for any errors, omissions, whether such errors or omissions result from negligence, accident, or any other cause or claims for loss or damages of any kind, including without limitation, indirect or consequential loss or damage arising out of use, inability to use, or about the reliability, accuracy or sufficiency of the information contained in this book.

Made with ❤ on the Notion Press Platform
www.notionpress.com

For my wife Madhuri

Contents

CHAPTER ONE

Emotional Intelligence

Emotional intelligence, often referred to as "EQ," is the ability to recognize, understand, and manage our own emotions, as well as the emotions of others. It is a vital skill for success in all areas of life, from personal relationships and career advancement, to overall well-being and happiness.

Emotional intelligence (EI) has been found to be a key factor in personal and professional success as well as overall well-being. People with high EI tend to be more resilient, better at handling stress, and more effective in relationships and at work.

EI can be developed and improved through training and practice. Some common techniques include mindfulness meditation, journaling, and coaching.

In this book, we will explore the concept of emotional intelligence in depth, examining the various components that make up EQ and how they can be developed and strengthened. We will delve into the science behind emotions and how they affect our behaviour and decision-making, as well as the ways in which emotions can be managed and regulated to improve overall well-being.

We will also look at the practical applications of emotional intelligence, including how it can be used to improve communication and relationships, increase empathy and compassion, and boost confidence and resilience. Through a combination of research, expert insights, and real-life examples, this book will provide you with a comprehensive understanding of emotional intelligence and the tools and strategies you need to develop your own EQ.

Whether you are looking to improve your personal or professional life or simply want to better understand and manage your emotions, this book is an essential guide to unlocking the power of emotional intelligence. So let's begin our journey together and discover the many ways in which EQ can help us live more fulfilling and meaningful lives.

What is an Emotionally Intelligent Attitude?

An emotionally intelligent attitude is the ability to recognise and understand one's own emotions and the emotions of others, as well as the ability to manage and regulate those emotions in a healthy and productive manner. This type of attitude is characterized by several key traits, such as self-awareness, empathy, emotional regulation, and effective communication.

Examples of an Emotionally Intelligent Attitude include:

- **Self-awareness** is the ability to recognise and comprehend one's own emotions, as well as their triggers and consequences.For example, recognising when you are feeling stressed and taking steps to manage that stress in a healthy way.
- **Empathy**: being able to understand and relate to the emotions of others, and responding in a supportive and compassionate manner. For example, recognising when a colleague is upset and offering to help or simply listening
- **Emotional regulation**: being able to manage and regulate one's emotions in a healthy and productive manner, rather than allowing them to control behavior. For example, instead of getting angry and lashing out, take a moment to calm down and then address the situation in a calm and rational manner.
- **Effective communication**: being able to express one's emotions in a clear and respectful manner, as well as being able to effectively listen and understand the emotions of others. For

example, instead of bottling up emotions and causing a misunderstanding, being able to express your feelings in a clear and constructive manner.

Overall, an emotionally intelligent attitude is characterised by the ability to recognise and understand emotions, as well as the ability to manage and regulate them in a healthy and productive manner. This type of attitude is essential for success in all areas of life, from personal relationships and career advancement, to overall well-being and happiness.

Why Emotionally Intelligent attitude is important?

Emotional intelligence is important because it enables us to navigate the complex and ever-changing landscape of human emotions and interactions. It allows us to better understand ourselves and others, and to respond to situations in a more effective and appropriate way.

Having a high level of emotional intelligence can also lead to improved communication and relationships, both in personal and professional settings. It can help us to build stronger connections with others, and to resolve conflicts and misunderstandings more effectively.

Additionally, emotional intelligence can have a positive impact on our overall well-being and mental health. It can help us to manage stress and difficult emotions, and to build resilience and inner strength.

In the professional sphere, emotionally intelligent individuals tend to be more successful in their careers.They are more likely to be able to manage relationships with colleagues and customers, negotiate effectively, and lead teams and organizations.

In short, emotional intelligence is a vital skill that enables us to live more fulfilling and meaningful lives, both personally and professionally. It is an essential tool for navigating the complex and ever-changing landscape of human emotions and interactions.

CHAPTER TWO

Emotional Intelligence: Attitudes and Behavior

Emotional intelligence attitudes and behaviours are the ways in which we demonstrate our understanding and management of emotions in our daily lives. These attitudes and behaviours are integral to the development and expression of emotional intelligence, and are essential for building strong relationships and achieving success in all areas of life.

Some key Emotional Intelligence Attitudes and Behaviours include:

- **Self-awareness**: being aware of one's own emotions and how they affect behaviour and decision-making.
- **Self-regulation**: being able to manage and regulate one's own emotions, rather than being controlled by them.
- **Motivation**: being driven to achieve goals and reach one's full potential, rather than being held back by negative emotions or a lack of motivation.
- **Empathy**: being able to understand and relate to the emotions of others, and to respond appropriately to their needs and feelings.
- **Social skills**: being able to communicate effectively and build positive relationships with others, through the use of appropriate emotional intelligence attitudes and behaviors.

These attitudes and behaviours can be learned, developed, and improved over time, through a combination of self-reflection, self-awareness, and practice. By cultivating and expressing these attitudes and behaviors, individuals can improve their emotional intelligence and achieve greater success and fulfilment in all areas of life.

Emotional intelligence is a combination of attitudes and behaviours that allow us to effectively recognize, understand, and manage our own emotions and the emotions of others. It encompasses a range of skills and abilities that are essential for success in all areas of life, from personal relationships to career advancement and overall well-being.

Attitudes play a crucial role in emotional intelligence, as they shape our perception of the world and influence our emotional responses. These attitudes include self-awareness, self-regulation, empathy, and motivation.

Self-awareness is the ability to recognise and understand our own emotions, thoughts, and feelings. It involves being aware of our strengths and weaknesses, and understanding how our emotions can affect our behaviour and decision-making.

Self-regulation is the ability to manage and control our own emotions, thoughts, and behaviors. It involves the ability to set and achieve goals, to manage stress, and to control impulses.

Empathy is the ability to understand and share the feelings of others. It involves being able to put ourselves in other people's shoes and respond to their emotions in a compassionate and understanding way.

Motivation is the drive to achieve our goals, and to better ourselves and the world around us. It is the fuel that drives emotional intelligence, and it is essential for personal and professional success.

Behavior also plays a crucial role in emotional intelligence, as it is the way in which we express and act on our emotions. Emotionally intelligent individuals tend to be able to communicate effectively, navigate relationships and interactions with ease, and make sound decisions based on their emotions and the emotions of others.

This book will delve into these attitudes and behaviours in depth, examining how they work together to shape our emotional intelligence and how they can be developed and strengthened to improve our overall well-being. With a combination of research, expert insights, and real-life examples, this book will provide you with the tools and strategies you need to understand and harness the power of emotional intelligence.

Developing the habits of Emotional Intelligence

Developing the habits of emotional intelligence is a process that requires time, effort, and a willingness to learn and grow. However, with the right mindset and approach, it is possible to improve your EQ and achieve greater success in all areas of life.

Here are a few habits that can help you develop your emotional intelligence:

- Practice self-awareness: Take time to reflect on your thoughts, feelings, and emotions. Understand how they affect your behaviour and decision-making.
- Learn to regulate your emotions: Practice techniques such as deep breathing and mindfulness to manage stress and control impulses.
- Cultivate empathy: Try to put yourself in other people's shoes and understand their perspectives. Practice active listening and show compassion and understanding toward others.
- Set goals and stay motivated: Identify what you want to achieve and create a plan to reach your goals. Stay motivated by focusing on the benefits of achieving your objectives.
- Communicate effectively: Learn to express yourself clearly and assertively. Practice active listening and work on building strong relationships with others.

- Reflect and Learn: Reflect on your experiences and learn from them. This will help you understand how your emotions and behaviour affected the outcome and how you can improve next time.
- Seek feedback from others and be open to it: Seek feedback from others and be open to constructive criticism. This can help you gain new perspectives and identify areas for improvement.

Remember, developing emotional intelligence is a lifelong journey. It requires patience, persistence, and a willingness to learn and grow. By incorporating these habits into your daily routine, you can improve your EQ and achieve greater success in all areas of your life.

How Emotional Intelligence helps with Pressure and Stress

Emotional intelligence plays a vital role in helping us to manage pressure and stress. It allows us to better understand and regulate our emotions, and to respond to challenging situations in a more effective and appropriate way.

One of the key aspects of emotional intelligence is self-awareness, which enables us to recognize and understand our emotions and how they affect our behavior and decision-making. By being aware of our emotions, we can better manage them, and avoid becoming overwhelmed by stress and pressure.

Self-regulation is another important aspect of emotional intelligence. It allows us to manage and control our emotions, thoughts, and behaviors, and to set and achieve goals. This can help us to stay calm and focused under pressure, and to manage stress in a more effective way.

Empathy is also an important aspect of emotional intelligence, as it allows us to understand and share the feelings of others. By being able to put ourselves in other people's shoes, we can respond to challenging situations in a more compassionate and understanding way, which can help to reduce stress and pressure.

Additionally, emotional intelligence can help us to build strong relationships and communicate effectively, which can provide a sense of support and understanding when dealing with stress and pressure.

Overall, emotional intelligence provides us with the tools and strategies we need to navigate the complex and ever-changing landscape of human emotions and interactions. By developing our emotional intelligence, we can improve our ability to manage stress and pressure, and to achieve greater success and well-being in all areas of life.

CHAPTER THREE

The Five Pillars of Emotional Intelligence

The Five Pillars or Competencies of Emotional Intelligence

The Five Pillars of Emotional Intelligence are:

- Self-awareness is defined as the ability to recognise and comprehend one's own emotions, strengths, weaknesses, needs, and drives.
- Self-regulation refers to the ability to control or redirect disruptive impulses and moods, as well as the ability to think before acting.
- Motivation: A passion to work for reasons that go beyond money or status and a propensity to pursue goals with energy and persistence.
- Empathy: is the ability to understand the emotional makeup of other people and the skill of treating them according to their emotional reactions.
- Social skills: proficiency in managing relationships and building networks, and an ability to find common ground and build rapport.

Self-Awareness and Self-Control

Self-awareness refers to the ability to have a clear understanding of one's own thoughts, feelings, and behaviors. This includes being able to recognise one's own emotions and how they affect one's actions, as well as being able to understand one's own mental processes. Self-awareness is an important aspect of emotional intelligence, as it allows individuals to manage their own emotions, as well as understand and respond to the emotions of others.

Self-control, on the other hand, refers to the ability to regulate one's own behavior, thoughts, and emotions. This includes being able to resist impulses and temptations, as well as being able to manage one's own emotional reactions. Self-control is an important aspect of impulse control, and it is closely related to the concept of willpower.

Both self-awareness and self-control are important for leading a successful and fulfilling life. Self-awareness allows individuals to understand their own thoughts and emotions, which in turn allows them to manage their own behaviour and reactions. Self-control allows individuals to resist impulses and temptations, which can help them make better decisions and achieve their goals.

The development of self-awareness and self-control begins in early childhood and continues throughout one's life. Parents and carers play an important role in helping children develop these skills by setting boundaries, providing guidance, and modelling appropriate behavior. As children grow and develop, they learn to recognise their own thoughts and feelings and begin to develop the ability to regulate their own behavior.

Education and socialisation also play a role in the development of self-awareness and self-control. Through interactions with others, children learn to understand and navigate social norms and expectations. They also learn to recognise and understand the emotions of others, which can help them develop empathy and improve their social skills.

In adulthood, self-awareness and self-control can be further developed through various practises such as mindfulness, meditation, and cognitive-behavioral therapy. These practises can help individuals become more aware of their thoughts, feelings, and behaviors, and develop strategies for managing them.

In conclusion, self-awareness and self-control are important aspects of emotional intelligence and impulse control. They are essential for leading a successful and fulfilling life, and their development begins in early childhood and continues throughout one's life. Education, socialization, and various practises can help individuals further develop these skills.

Social Skills and Empathy

Social skills and empathy are two important pillars of emotional intelligence.

Social skills refer to proficiency in managing relationships and building networks, as well as the ability to find common ground and build rapport with others. It includes being able to communicate effectively, negotiate, resolve conflicts, and lead others. Good social skills are essential for building strong relationships in both personal and professional settings. It also enables individuals to navigate social situations, understand the perspectives of others, and build trust and cooperation.

Empathy, on the other hand, is the ability to understand the emotional makeup of other people and the skill of treating them according to their emotional reactions. It involves being able to put oneself in someone else's shoes, to understand their emotions and perspective, and to respond in a way that is sensitive to their needs. Empathy is essential for building strong relationships, as it enables individuals to understand and relate to others, and to build trust and cooperation.

Empathy and social skills are closely related. Empathy allows individuals to understand the perspectives of others, and social skills enable individuals to respond in a way that is sensitive to those perspectives. Together, empathy and social skills allow individuals to build strong relationships, understand and relate to others, and navigate social situations.

Good social skills and empathy also make an individual an effective leader, team player, and collaborator. Empathy allows leaders to understand the needs and emotions of their team members and respond accordingly. It also serves to motivate and inspire them.Social skills enable leaders to build trust and cooperation among team members, resolve conflicts, and communicate effectively.

In the workplace, social skills and empathy are essential for building effective teams and creating a positive work environment. Empathy allows individuals to understand and relate to their colleagues, while social skills enable them to build trust and cooperate. This helps to create a positive work environment where individuals feel valued, respected, and engaged.

Social skills and empathy also play an important role in customer service and sales. Empathy allows customer service representatives and salespeople to understand and relate to the needs and emotions of their customers. This, in turn, helps them to build trust and establish a positive relationship with their customers. Social skills enable them to communicate effectively, resolve conflicts, and negotiate effectively.

In conclusion, social skills and empathy are two important pillars of emotional intelligence that are essential for building strong relationships, navigating social situations, and achieving success in personal and professional settings. Social skills enable individuals to communicate effectively, resolve conflicts, and build networks, while empathy allows them to understand and relate to the emotions and perspectives of others. Together, they play a critical role in emotional intelligence and are essential for personal growth and development.

Self-Motivation

Self-motivation is the ability to initiate and maintain effort towards achieving a goal, even in the face of obstacles or setbacks. It is an essential component of emotional intelligence, as it allows individuals to regulate their own emotions and behaviours in order to achieve their goals.

Emotional intelligence is the ability to recognize, understand, and manage one's own emotions, as well as the emotions of others. It involves several key components, including self-awareness, self-regulation, motivation, empathy, and social skills. Self-motivation is closely related to self-regulation, as it involves the ability to initiate and maintain effort towards a goal despite emotional challenges.

Self-motivation is important for achieving success in various areas of life, including work, education, and personal relationships. Individuals who are self-motivated are able to set goals for themselves and take the necessary steps to achieve them. They are also able to persist in the face of obstacles and setbacks, which allows them to overcome challenges and achieve their goals.

The development of self-motivation begins in childhood and continues throughout one's life. Parents and carers play an important role in helping children develop self-motivation by setting clear expectations, providing encouragement, and offering opportunities for children to take on responsibilities. Children who are given opportunities to make choices and take on responsibilities are more likely to develop self-motivation.

Education and socialisation also play a role in the development of self-motivation. Through interactions with others, children learn to understand and navigate social norms and expectations. They also learn to recognise and understand the emotions of others, which can help them develop empathy and improve their social skills.

In adulthood, self-motivation can be further developed through various practises such as goal-setting, mindfulness, and cognitive-behavioral therapy. Setting specific, measurable, achievable, relevant, and time-bound (SMART) goals can help individuals focus their efforts and increase their motivation. Mindfulness and meditation can help individuals become more aware of their thoughts and emotions and develop strategies for managing them. Cognitive-behavioral therapy can help individuals identify and change negative thought patterns that may be hindering their motivation.

Emotional intelligence plays a significant role in self-motivation as well. Individuals with high emotional intelligence are better able to recognise and understand their own emotions and the emotions of others. They are also better able to regulate their own emotions, which allows them to persist in the face of obstacles and setbacks. Moreover, they are better able to empathise with others, which allows them to understand and navigate social norms and expectations.

In Short, self-motivation is the ability to initiate and maintain effort towards achieving a goal, even in the face of obstacles or setbacks. It is an essential component of emotional intelligence and plays a significant role in achieving success in various areas of life. The development of self-motivation begins in childhood and continues throughout one's life. Education, socialization, and various practises such as goal-setting, mindfulness, and cognitive-behavioral therapy can help individuals further develop self-motivation. Emotional intelligence also plays a crucial role in self-motivation, as individuals with high emotional intelligence are better able to recognise and understand their own emotions, regulate their own emotions, and empathise with others, which ultimately leads them to persist in the face of obstacles and setbacks to achieve their goals.

CHAPTER FOUR

Harnessing Emotional Intelligence

Harnessing emotional intelligence involves developing the ability to recognize, understand, and manage one's own emotions, as well as the emotions of others. Here are a few ways to harness emotional intelligence:

- Practice self-awareness: This involves understanding your own emotions and how they influence your thoughts and behaviors. One way to do this is through mindfulness and meditation, which can help you become more aware of your thoughts and emotions in the present moment.
- Develop self-regulation: This involves the ability to manage your own emotions and behaviour in order to achieve your goals. One way to do this is through goal-setting and making a plan to achieve your goals.
- Enhance empathy: This involves understanding and being able to relate to the emotions of others. One way to do this is through active listening and putting yourself in other people's shoes.
- Improve social skills: This involves the ability to communicate and interact with others effectively. One way to do this is through practice, such as role-playing or participating in social activities.
- Seek feedback: This involves getting feedback from others on your emotional intelligence skills and how you can improve

them.

- Learn from experience: This involves reflecting on past experiences and identifying how your emotions and actions influenced the outcome.
- Read, watch, or listen to content related to emotional intelligence: This involves reading books, watching videos, or listening to podcasts that provide information on emotional intelligence and how to develop it.
- Seek professional help: If you find it difficult to develop your emotional intelligence on your own, consider seeking help from a therapist or counselor.

It's important to note that emotional intelligence is not a fixed trait and that it can be developed over time through consistent effort and practice. It's also important to remember that emotional intelligence is a multidimensional construct and that different aspects of it can be developed at different rates.

How Emotional Intelligence helps prevent Stress and Fatigue

Emotional intelligence can help prevent stress and fatigue by providing individuals with the tools to recognize, understand, and manage their own emotions, as well as the emotions of others. Here are a few ways emotional intelligence can help prevent stress and fatigue:

- Self-awareness: Emotionally intelligent individuals are better able to recognise their own emotional states, which allows them to identify when they are becoming stressed or fatigued. Once they recognise these states, they can take steps to manage them before they become overwhelming.
- Self-regulation: Emotionally intelligent individuals are better able to manage their own emotions and behaviours, which allows them to avoid becoming overwhelmed by stress and

fatigue. They are able to set realistic goals, prioritise their tasks, and manage their time effectively.

- Empathy: Emotionally intelligent individuals are better able to understand and relate to the emotions of others, which allows them to navigate social interactions more effectively. This can help reduce the stress and fatigue that can come from conflicts and misunderstandings with others.
- Social skills: Emotionally intelligent individuals are better able to communicate and interact with others effectively, which can help reduce the stress and fatigue that can come from social interactions. They are able to build and maintain positive relationships, which can provide support and reduce stress.
- Resilience: Emotionally intelligent individuals are better able to bounce back from stress and setbacks. They are able to maintain a positive outlook even in the face of adversity. which can help reduce stress and fatigue.
- Emotionally intelligent individuals are better able to control their reactions to stressors, they can choose how to respond to stressors instead of just reacting to them. This can help them avoid the negative effects of stress, such as fatigue, anxiety, or depression.
- Emotionally intelligent individuals are better able to manage their work-life balance, which can help them prevent stress and fatigue caused by overwork.

Emotional intelligence also includes being able to recognise the signs of stress and fatigue in oneself and taking preventive measures to avoid reaching a state where they're harder to manage. Emotionally intelligent individuals are better equipped to handle stress and fatigue in a healthy and effective way.

How Emotional Intelligence helps with Career and Success

Emotional intelligence can play a significant role in career and success by providing individuals with the skills and abilities to navigate the social and emotional aspects of their work environment. Here are a few ways emotional intelligence can help with career success:

- Self-awareness: Emotionally intelligent individuals are better able to understand their own strengths, weaknesses, and values, which can help them make informed career decisions and set realistic goals.
- Self-regulation: Emotionally intelligent individuals are better able to manage their own emotions and behaviours, which can help them stay focused and motivated in the face of obstacles and challenges. They are able to adapt and change course when necessary.
- Empathy: Emotionally intelligent individuals are better able to understand and relate to the emotions of others, which can help them build strong relationships and communicate effectively with colleagues, supervisors, and clients.
- Social skills: Emotionally intelligent individuals are better able to communicate, collaborate, and lead effectively, which can help them build strong teams and achieve common goals. They are able to build trust and respect with others, which can help them achieve success in their careers.
- Leadership: Emotionally intelligent individuals have the ability to inspire and motivate others, which can be crucial for success in leadership roles. They are able to create a positive and productive work environment, which can lead to better performance from employees.
- Problem-solving: Emotionally intelligent individuals are better able to manage conflict, which can help them resolve problems and make better decisions. They are able to consider multiple perspectives and emotions to come up with a better solution.
- Resilience: Emotionally intelligent individuals are better able to bounce back from setbacks and challenges, which can help them

maintain their motivation and focus on their goals. They are able to maintain a positive outlook and adapt to changes.

- Emotionally intelligent individuals are better able to manage their work-life balance, which can help them avoid burnout and maintain their productivity.

In summary, emotional intelligence can help individuals navigate the social and emotional aspects of their work environment and build strong relationships, communicate effectively, and lead and inspire others. It can also help to promote a positive and productive work environment, which can lead to better performance, problem-solving, and ultimately career success. Emotionally intelligent individuals are better equipped to handle the challenges and stress that come with a career and are better placed to achieve success.

CHAPTER FIVE

Applied Emotional Intelligence

Applied emotional intelligence refers to the practical application of emotional intelligence skills in various settings, such as the workplace, in relationships, or in personal development. Here are a few ways emotional intelligence can be applied:

- **In the workplace**: emotionally intelligent individuals can apply their skills to improve communication, collaboration, and leadership. They can build strong relationships with colleagues, clients, and supervisors, and create a positive and productive work environment. They can also use their emotional intelligence to manage stress and conflict in the workplace.
- **In relationships**: emotionally intelligent individuals can apply their skills to improve communication, empathy, and understanding in their personal relationships. They can build stronger, more fulfilling relationships by understanding the emotional needs of others and expressing their own emotions effectively.
- **In personal development**: emotionally intelligent individuals can use their skills to improve self-awareness, self-regulation, and resilience. They can set realistic goals, manage their time and emotions, and bounce back from setbacks. They can also use emotional intelligence to manage stress and maintain a positive outlook.

- **Emotionally** intelligent individuals can apply their skills in a coaching or mentoring role, helping others to develop their emotional intelligence and improve their performance and well-being.
- **In Education**: Emotionally intelligent individuals can apply their skills in education by using their emotional intelligence to create a positive learning environment and build strong relationships with students and colleagues. They can also use emotional intelligence to manage stress and conflict and support the emotional well-being of students.
- **In healthcare**, emotionally intelligent individuals can apply their skills by using their emotional intelligence to build strong relationships with patients and colleagues, manage stress and conflict, and support the emotional well-being of patients.
- **In therapy**: emotionally intelligent individuals can use their skills to improve communication, empathy, and understanding. They can help clients understand and manage their emotions, set realistic goals, and develop resilience.
- Emotionally intelligent individuals can apply their skills in various fields such as management, sales, customer service, and more.

Emotional intelligence can be applied in various settings to improve communication, relationships, personal development, and performance. Emotionally intelligent individuals are better equipped to navigate the social and emotional aspects of their work and personal lives and to achieve their goals.

Self-monitoring and Positive Change

Self-monitoring is the process of observing and recording one's own behavior, thoughts, and emotions. It is a powerful tool that can be used to make positive changes in one's life. Through self-monitoring, individuals can gain a better understanding of their habits, behaviors, and thoughts, and use this information to make positive changes in their lives.

One of the most important aspects of self-monitoring is the ability to identify patterns in one's behavior. For example, an individual may realise that they tend to overeat when they are feeling stressed or anxious. By recognizing this pattern, they can take steps to address the underlying cause of their overeating, such as finding healthier ways to cope with stress.

Another benefit of self-monitoring is the ability to set and track progress toward specific goals. For example, an individual may set a goal to exercise for 30 minutes each day, and use self-monitoring to track their progress towards this goal. This can help to keep them motivated and on track, and it can also provide a sense of accomplishment when they reach their goal.

Self-monitoring can also be used to improve self-awareness and self-regulation. By observing and recording one's own behavior, thoughts, and emotions, individuals can gain a better understanding of themselves and their triggers. This can help them identify negative patterns and make positive changes in their behavior. For example, an individual may realise that they tend to become easily irritated when they are tired and use this knowledge to plan their day in a way that allows them to get enough sleep.

In addition to these benefits, self-monitoring can also be used to improve communication with others. By understanding one's own behaviour and thoughts, individuals can communicate more effectively with others and build stronger relationships. For example, an individual may recognise that they tend to become defensive when criticized, and use this knowledge to work on becoming more open to feedback.

Overall, self-monitoring is a powerful tool that can be used to make positive changes in one's life. It can help individuals identify patterns in their behavior, set and track progress towards goals, improve self-awareness and self-regulation, and improve communication with others. By using self-monitoring, individuals can gain a better understanding of themselves and take steps to improve their lives.

In conclusion, self-monitoring is an essential tool for personal development and positive change. It allows individuals to take a step back and assess their own behavior, thoughts, and emotions and make necessary adjustments. By keeping track of their progress, individuals can stay motivated and on track towards achieving their goals. With self-awareness, self-regulation, and improved communication, individuals can improve their relationships and overall well-being. Self-monitoring is a valuable tool that can be used by anyone looking to make positive changes in their life.

Helping and Supporting Others

Helping and supporting others is a key component of emotional intelligence. This is because emotional intelligence requires individuals to have empathy, understanding, and the ability to connect with others. When a person helps or supports someone else, they are able to put themselves in the other person's shoes, understand their perspective, and offer the kind of assistance that is needed. This requires a level of emotional intelligence that is not possible for those who are not in tune with their own emotions or the emotions of others.

Furthermore, helping and supporting others can also help individuals improve their emotional intelligence by providing opportunities for personal growth and self-reflection. For example, when a person helps someone else with a difficult problem, they may need to assess their own emotional reactions and find ways to manage their own stress and frustration. By doing this, individuals can learn more about their own emotions and develop the skills needed to manage their own emotions more effectively.

Moreover, helping and supporting others can also improve emotional intelligence by increasing self-awareness and emotional regulation. When individuals are engaged in helping others, they are able to practise emotional regulation in a supportive and safe environment, which can help them develop better skills in this area. Additionally, by helping others, individuals are able to reflect on their own emotions and gain a deeper understanding of their own emotional experiences, which can lead to increased self-awareness.

Overall, helping and supporting others is a key component of emotional intelligence, as it requires individuals to understand, connect with, and respond to others in a way that is emotionally intelligent and supportive. By doing this, people can raise their emotional intelligence and gain the ability to better manage difficult emotional situations.

CHAPTER SIX

Ways to Keep Improving your Emotional Intelligence

Study Humility

Humility is an essential component of emotional intelligence. It involves recognising one's own limitations and being open to feedback and learning from others. When combined with emotional intelligence, humility can help individuals better understand and manage their own emotions and behaviors, and improve their relationships with others.

To study humility while improving emotional intelligence, individuals can start by practising self-awareness. This may involve reflecting on one's own thoughts, emotions, and behaviours and understanding how they affect others.

Next, individuals can work on building empathy by putting themselves in other people's shoes and trying to understand their perspectives. This can be done by actively listening to others, reading books or articles, or participating in empathy exercises.

In addition, individuals can practise humility by being open to feedback and learning from others. This may entail seeking constructive criticism, listening to other people's points of view, and learning from past mistakes..

It's also important to develop strong relationships based on trust, mutual respect, and open communication. This can be accomplished by actively listening, providing and receiving feedback, and being honest with others.

Furthermore, individuals can practise humility by admitting when they don't know something and seeking out knowledge from others. This may involve reading books, attending workshops, or talking to experts in a particular field.

Finally, practising stress management techniques such as deep breathing, meditation, or yoga can also help to improve emotional intelligence and humility.

In conclusion, humility is a key component of emotional intelligence and can help individuals better understand and manage their own emotions and behaviors, and improve their relationships with others. By practising self-awareness, building empathy, seeking feedback, developing strong relationships, seeking knowledge, and practising stress management, individuals can study humility and improve their emotional intelligence.

Notice how you react to people.

When working on improving emotional intelligence, it's important to pay attention to how you react to people. This includes observing your own thoughts, emotions, and behaviour when interacting with others. Here are some tips for noticing and improving your reactions to people:

- Take note of your emotions: When interacting with others, pay attention to how you feel. Are you feeling angry, frustrated, or anxious? Identifying your emotions will help you understand why you're reacting in a certain way.
- Observe your behavior: Notice how you respond to others when you're feeling a certain way. Are you becoming defensive or shutting down? This can be a sign that you're not handling your

emotions well.

- Identify triggers: Try to identify what triggers your reactions to people. Is it a specific person, situation, or type of behavior? Understanding your triggers can help you avoid them in the future.
- Practice active listening: When interacting with others, practise active listening. This means truly listening to what the other person is saying without interrupting or thinking about your response.
- Take a step back: If you find yourself becoming reactive, take a step back and take a break from the interaction. This can give you time to cool down and process your emotions.
- Practice empathy: Try to put yourself in the other person's shoes and understand their perspective. This can help you respond in a more compassionate and understanding way.
- Reflect on your reactions: After interacting with others, take some time to reflect on your reactions. Think about what you could have done differently, and come up with a plan for how you'll handle similar situations in the future.
- Seek feedback: Ask others for feedback on how you interact with them, try to understand their perception of you.
- Seek professional help: If you're struggling to improve your reactions to people, seek help from a therapist or counselor. They can provide guidance and support to help you develop the skills you need.

Remember that improving emotional intelligence takes time and practice, be patient and try to learn from your mistakes.

Look honestly at how you think about, and interact with others.

To improve emotional intelligence, it's important to look honestly at how you think about and interact with others. This may involve examining your own biases, prejudices, and assumptions and being willing to challenge and change them.

One way to do this is by becoming more aware of your own emotions and how they affect your interactions with others. For example, if you tend to become defensive when criticized, try to understand the underlying emotions that are driving this behaviour and work on managing them in a healthier way.

Another important aspect of improving emotional intelligence is learning to empathise with others. This means actively trying to understand other people's perspectives and feelings and recognising that everyone's experience is different. Try to put yourself in others' shoes, and try to understand where they are coming from.

It's also important to work on building strong relationships with others. Strong relationships are built on trust, mutual respect, and open communication. Practice active listening, give and receive feedback, and be honest with others.

Finally, effective communication is key to building strong relationships. Practice active listening, give and receive feedback, and use "I" statements to express your feelings. Try to avoid blaming or accusing others when communicating; instead, focus on understanding and finding a solution.

Overall, improving emotional intelligence involves looking honestly at your own behaviour and interactions with others and being willing to challenge and change them. This may involve becoming more self-aware, managing your emotions, empathising with others, building strong relationships, and communicating effectively. Remember to be patient with yourself; emotional intelligence is a lifelong process that takes time to develop.

Do a Self-Evaluation.

Conducting a self-evaluation can be a valuable tool for improving emotional intelligence. Here are some steps to guide you through the process:

- Reflect on your current level of emotional intelligence. Think about your ability to recognise and understand your own emotions, as well as the emotions of others. Consider how well you are able to manage your emotions and how effectively you communicate with others.
- Identify areas for improvement: Based on your reflection, identify specific areas where you would like to improve your emotional intelligence. For example, you may want to work on managing your stress or improving your empathy.
- Set specific goals: For each area identified, set specific, measurable goals that you can work toward. For example, you may set a goal to practise mindfulness for 15 minutes each day to improve your ability to manage stress.
- Create a plan of action: Develop a plan of action that will help you achieve your goals. This may include specific steps, such as seeking professional help or reading books on emotional intelligence.
- Monitor your progress: Keep track of your progress by regularly monitoring your behaviour and emotions. Use self-monitoring tools, such as a journal or a mood tracker, to help you stay on track.
- Seek feedback: Seek feedback from others. Ask friends and family to give you honest feedback on your emotional intelligence and how you are doing.
- Reflect and adjust: reflect on your progress and make adjustments as needed. If you find that you are not making progress in a certain area, reassess your approach and consider seeking additional support.
- Be patient: Remember that improving emotional intelligence is a lifelong process; don't be hard on yourself if you don't see results overnight; be patient and keep working on it.

By conducting a self-evaluation, setting specific goals, and monitoring your progress, you can take an active role in improving your emotional intelligence. Remember to seek feedback, be patient, and adjust your approach as needed. With time and effort, you will see improvement.

Manage your Emotions.

Managing emotions is an essential part of maintaining a healthy and balanced life. Emotions are a natural part of being human, and it is important to learn how to handle them in a healthy way. The first step in managing emotions is to understand them. Emotions are not good or bad; they are simply a response to a situation or a feeling. Understanding what triggers certain emotions can help you identify and manage them better.

One way to manage emotions is through mindfulness. Mindfulness is the practise of being present in the moment and paying attention to your thoughts, feelings, and bodily sensations. By practising mindfulness, you can learn to observe your emotions without getting caught up in them. This can help you understand your emotions better and respond to them in a calm and rational way.

Another way to manage emotions is through self-care. Taking care of yourself physically, mentally, and emotionally can help you feel more balanced and in control of your emotions. This can include activities such as exercise, meditation, and journaling. It can also include setting boundaries and taking time for yourself.

Finally, it is important to communicate your emotions effectively. Being able to express your emotions in a healthy way can help you build stronger relationships and feel more understood. This can include talking to a therapist or counselor or talking to a loved one.

In conclusion, managing emotions is an important part of maintaining a healthy and balanced life. By understanding your emotions, practising mindfulness, taking care of yourself, and communicating effectively, you can learn to handle your emotions in a healthy way. Remember that emotions are a natural part of being human, and it is important to learn how to handle them in a healthy way.

Take Responsibility for your Behavior.

Taking responsibility for your behaviour is crucial for building emotional intelligence. Emotional intelligence is the ability to understand, manage, and express emotions in a healthy way. It involves being aware of your own emotions and the emotions of others and being able to regulate your own emotions in a way that is appropriate for the situation.

By taking responsibility for your behavior, you can build emotional intelligence by:

- Understanding your emotions: By taking responsibility for your behavior, you are acknowledging that your actions and decisions have an impact on your emotions. This allows you to understand the connection between your behaviour and your emotions, and to make conscious choices that align with your values and goals.
- Managing your emotions: When you take responsibility for your behavior, you are also taking responsibility for managing your emotions. This means being able to recognise when you are feeling overwhelmed or stressed and taking steps to regulate your emotions in a healthy way.
- Communicating effectively: Taking responsibility for your behaviour also means being able to communicate your emotions effectively. This entails being able to express your emotions in a situation-appropriate manner while also respecting the emotions of others.
- Building empathy: When you take responsibility for your behavior, you are also building empathy. This means being able to understand and relate to the emotions of others, which is crucial for building healthy relationships.

In conclusion, taking responsibility for your behaviour is crucial for building emotional intelligence. It involves being aware of your own emotions, managing them in a healthy way, communicating effectively, and building empathy. By taking responsibility for your behavior, you can build emotional intelligence and improve your overall well-being.

Be open and sociable.

Being open and sociable is an important aspect of building emotional intelligence. Emotional intelligence is the ability to recognize, understand, and manage our own emotions, as well as the emotions of others. By being open and sociable, we can build stronger relationships, better understand the emotions of others, and learn to manage our own emotions more effectively.

Being open and sociable means being willing to engage with others and to share your thoughts and feelings. This can include actively listening to others and being willing to share your own thoughts and feelings in return. It also means being willing to be vulnerable and to open up about your own emotions, which can help others to understand you better and to build stronger relationships.

Being sociable also means being willing to try new things and to step out of your comfort zone. This can include meeting new people, trying new activities, and taking part in different social events. By being open to new experiences, you can learn more about yourself and others, and gain a better understanding of the emotions that drive different behaviours.

Finally, being open and sociable means being willing to learn from others. This can include learning from the experiences of others and being open to feedback. By learning from others, you can gain a better understanding of yourself and others, and learn to manage your own emotions more effectively.

In conclusion, being open and sociable is an important aspect of building emotional intelligence. By engaging with others, sharing your thoughts and feelings, trying new things, and learning from others, you can build stronger relationships, better understand the emotions of others, and learn to manage your own emotions more effectively. Remember that emotional intelligence is a skill that can be developed and improved over time.

Here are some additional ways to boost your Emotional Intelligence.

- Self-awareness: Improving your self-awareness is the foundation of emotional intelligence. This means being aware of your own emotions, their triggers, and how they affect your behavior. You can improve your self-awareness by practising mindfulness, journaling, and seeking feedback from others.
- Emotional regulation: being able to regulate your emotions in a healthy way is crucial for emotional intelligence. This means being able to manage your emotions, rather than allowing them to control you. You can improve your emotional regulation by practising stress management techniques such as deep breathing, meditation, and exercise.
- Empathy: Empathy is the ability to understand and relate to the emotions of others. You can improve your empathy by actively listening to others, trying to see things from their perspective, and practising active compassion.
- Social skills: Social skills are important for emotional intelligence, as they allow you to communicate effectively and build healthy relationships. Learn effective communication techniques, practise active listening, and develop your active listening skills to improve your social skills.
- Continuous learning: Emotional intelligence is not a fixed trait and can always be improved. Continuously learning about emotions and how to manage them is crucial for maintaining and improving emotional intelligence.
- Seek professional help if needed: Because emotional intelligence can be challenging to develop and maintain, seeking professional help from a therapist or counsellor can be beneficial.

- Practice self-awareness: Take the time to reflect on your own emotions and thoughts and understand how they affect your behavior. Try journaling, meditating, or talking to a therapist to help you gain a deeper understanding of yourself.
- Learn to manage your emotions: Develop strategies for managing your emotions in a healthy way. This may include practising mindfulness, deep breathing, or positive self-talk.
- Increase empathy: Practice putting yourself in other people's shoes, and try to understand their perspectives. Listen actively, and try to understand where they are coming from.
- Build strong relationships: Strong relationships are built on trust, mutual respect, and open communication. Practice active listening, give and receive feedback, and be honest with others.
- Learn to communicate effectively. Good communication is key to building strong relationships. Practice active listening, give and receive feedback, and use "I" statements to express your feelings.
- Practice stress management: Stress can have a negative impact on emotional intelligence. Learn to manage stress through techniques such as deep breathing, meditation, or yoga.
- Seek professional help: If you are struggling to improve your emotional intelligence, seek help from a therapist or counselor. They can provide guidance and support to help you develop the skills you need.
- Read and Learn: Keep learning about emotional intelligence and its related topics, read books, articles, and research papers to understand more about the topic.
- Practice what you learn: Try to put into practise what you learn. Set small goals and try to achieve them. Self-monitoring will help you understand your progress.
- Be patient: Improving your emotional intelligence is a lifelong process. Don't expect to see results overnight; be patient and keep working on it.

In conclusion, emotional intelligence is a set of skills that can be developed and improved over time. By focusing on self-awareness, emotional regulation, empathy, social skills, continuous learning, and seeking professional help if needed, you can improve your emotional intelligence and your overall well-being.

CHAPTER SEVEN

Summary

Emotional Intelligence is a book that explores the concept of emotional intelligence and how it can be used to improve overall well-being. The book delves into the importance of self-awareness, emotional regulation, empathy, and social skills in developing emotional intelligence. It also provides practical techniques for improving these skills, such as mindfulness, journaling, and stress management.

Throughout the book, the author emphasises the importance of continuous learning and self-reflection in developing and maintaining emotional intelligence. The author also highlights the importance of seeking professional help if needed, and how it can be beneficial in some cases.

The book is aimed at individuals looking to improve their emotional intelligence and overall well-being. It provides an in-depth understanding of emotional intelligence and practical tools for improving these skills. The author has written in a clear and concise manner, making the concepts discussed in the book simple to understand and apply.

The book also covers the connection between emotional intelligence and success in personal and professional life, and how it can be used to build stronger relationships and create a more fulfilling life.

In summary, Emotional Intelligence is an informative and practical guide that provides an in-depth understanding of emotional intelligence and how it can be used to improve overall well-being.The author offers practical tools and techniques for developing and maintaining emotional intelligence, making this book a valuable resource for anyone looking to improve their emotional intelligence and overall well-being.

www.ingramcontent.com/pod-product-compliance
Lightning Source LLC
Chambersburg PA
CBHW022123150726
47990CB00003B/1482